MW00975419

Scripture quotations have been taken from the New American Bible, Revised Edition (NABRE) from the USCCB website. www.usccb.org/bible

Cover art: *Rowing to rescue shipwrecked sailors off the Northumberland Coast* by James Wilson Carmichael

This work is free of known copyright restrictions.

Cover Photo by Joel Bengs on Unsplash.com

Mary Tillotson, editor
Fr. Anthony Smela, cover design, support, and good music enthusiast

ISBN-13: 978-1-387-92917-7

Printed by www.lulu.com

To the people of St. Hamm's,
You know the good you did.

Special Thanks to Fr. Bill Ashbaugh,
You're a gift from God to so many.

To Samuel Oliver,
who trusts our loving God to express
Himself in our group conscience.

About this Book:

From the beginning of humanity, we people have been bringing ourselves to ruin. And for as long as we have been bringing ourselves to ruin, God has been with us, helping us, loving us, and rescuing us.

You and I are probably surprised to see how far we have fallen, but God is not surprised. He has always known we would need Him right now. He has always and forever planned to meet us in this moment. If we let Him, God will rescue us.

Those of us in addiction recovery need to know: we are not alone among humanity; our story is not uncommon in history; we're not beyond the help of God; and God has been rescuing His ruined people since the beginning of time.

This book is a proclamation of this truth.

This book is a spiritual, Scriptural guide to the 12 Steps of recovery. It makes sense that Scripture and Steps can be brought together as a way to proclaim God's rescue. The Bible is the Living-Word story of God rescuing His people from self-ruination. The 12 Steps are a recovery path that leads to God. This book is not meant to be a 12 Step recovery how-to. It is by no means a replacement to the *Big Book of Alcoholics Anonymous* or *Twelve Steps, Twelve Traditions*. This book is intended to be a spiritual, Biblical help for people in recovery to enter into God the Father's rescue mission, as it is revealed and accomplished in God the Son, Jesus Christ. The Scriptures in this book are designed to help the reader move away from misunderstandings of God and begin to move into an understanding of God as He revealed Himself in Jesus. God is who He says He is, and He offers you and me a relationship of rescue and love.

So, it isn't necessary that you, Reader, begin this journey calling yourself a Christian. It isn't even necessary that you're a member of a particular recovery fellowship or practice a particular way of working the 12 Steps. If you've experienced the terrible crisis of needing rescue, this book is for you. If you want reassurance that you are included in God's rescue mission, this book is for you.

Each chapter of the book focuses on a single Step of recovery. With each Step I propose a Principle and a Reality, and I offer a brief reflection on the Step. I've chosen a few Scripture verses related to the Step (verses from both the Old and New Testaments); and I include a short commentary on the Scripture itself. Each chapter includes a workbook or journal reflection and discussion prompts. Each chapter concludes with a proclamation, a statement of God and His work.

You will notice, throughout *The Rescue*, the recovery steps have been reformatted into "I" and "me" statements so you, the Reader, can begin to experience in a deeply personal way God's love for you. For the most part, though, out of respect for the 12 Steps of Alcoholics Anonymous, the verb tenses of the original texts remain.

A note about notes: You will notice this book leaves a lot of space for you to write. Go ahead! Write in this book! Take notes, write reflections – not only of your experience, strength, and hope, but of others' insights and sharing, too.

About 'Rescue' Meetings:

People will come to our meetings from different recovery groups and with different understandings of the Steps. People will embrace different definitions of what qualifies as 'abstinent from addiction.' At our meetings, we do not argue about any of these things. Instead, we receive others' perspectives with a spirit of acceptance.

Certainly, it will seem natural to talk about the addictions from which God is rescuing us. But at 'Rescue' meetings, it isn't necessary that we introduce ourselves as our addictions. It is very acceptable to say, "My name is _____. I'm a child of God." or "Hi, my name is _____, and God is rescuing me." Or even just, "My name is _____." We confine our sharing to "I" statements and "God" statements. Crosstalk is reserved for the single purpose of identifying with another person's experience. Each of us shares our personal experience, strength, and hope. We believe others will learn more from that than from corrections or arguments.

We also come together with different levels of familiarity and knowledge of the Bible. At our meetings, we don't teach Scripture, and we don't Bible surf. Our table leaders are not to be viewed as Scripture experts or spiritual directors; their role is to keep the discussion on task and the tone welcoming to all who attend. Though the harmony of Scripture is a beautiful thing, at our meetings, we confine our attention *only* to those Scriptures proposed in the chapter we're working. Sometimes a person will come with theological interpretations of the Bible which differ from another person's interpretation. These differences usually reflect views espoused by various denominations. Again, we do not argue, and we do not correct. Of course, there are truer and less true understandings of God as He is revealed in Scripture, but our intention here is not to wrestle with theology, important as that may be. Our intention here is to *enter into* the Living Word of God and to let His Word bring each of us into an ever-deepening encounter with Jesus Christ, God the Son.

Unlike typical 12 Step groups, "Rescue" groups don't count abstinence time. Our measure of success is whether we are working the Steps *today*, and whether we are meeting God in His Living word and through prayer *today*.

In other words, the purpose of our meeting time is to gather as people being rescued by God, to spend time in His Living Word, to let His Word transform each of us, and to share the good work God is doing in us.

Finally, a word about sponsorship:

Typically, 12 Step recovery success relies heavily on the sponsor-sponsee relationship. *The Rescue: A 12 Step Bible Study*, is structured differently because most of us are not Bible scholars, priests, ordained ministers, or qualified spiritual directors. Therefore, we do not sponsor each other on the Rescue journey. Instead, we accompany each other; we pray together; we share our experiences of God rescuing us. We encourage people who want a formal guide through Scripture to seek out a validly qualified individual.

I hope and pray that by journeying into the Living Word of God, you and I approach the very heart of God. May we trust that we're being rescued by God!

Let us begin. *Father, send Your Holy Spirit. In Jesus' name we pray. Amen.*

NOTES

Step 1

**I admitted I was powerless over my addiction —
that my life had become unmanageable.**

Reality: Ruin
Principles: Honesty, Admission

All throughout history, human beings have brought themselves to ruin in many ways and by many means. To be brought to ruin means I have shattered my relationship with my community. It means I have broken my relationship with myself. I have smashed my relationship with God. I may also be penniless, homeless, and jobless. Maybe now, I'm even physically sick.

All throughout history ruined human beings have been restored by the goodness, the caring, and the providence (providing) of God. Not every ruined person is restored, but only because some refuse His help. But God is *able* to restore every ruined person. He *desires* to restore every ruined, broken person. But the ruined person first has to know he or she is ruined. I have to admit it. Admitting the devastating truth of my ruination is the first step that will begin to set me free.

We pray: Heavenly Father, Abba, Your Word is alive. Let Your Word be alive in me. Come Holy Spirit. In Jesus' name I pray. Amen.

Read the Scripture verses slowly:

Psalm 69:3   I have sunk into the mire of the deep, where there is no foothold. I have gone down to the watery depths; the flood overwhelms me.

What word or phrase stands out to me?

Isaiah 1:7   Your country is waste, your cities burnt with fire; Your land before your eyes strangers devour it…

What word or phrase stands out to me?

2 Chronicles 36:19   They burnt the house of God, tore down the walls of Jerusalem, burnt down all its palaces, and destroyed all its precious objects.

What word or phrase stands out to me?

Job 22:16   They were snatched before their time; their foundations a river swept away…

What word or phrase stands out to me?

All of these passages are from the Old Testament. They were written at various times in ancient history; all of them are thousands of years old. The psalms were written by King David, the second King of Israel. He was beloved, chosen, and anointed by God, but his sins caused him great calamity and distress. Job's story is a dramatic story of human suffering. He didn't bring terrible suffering upon himself, but his friends thought God was punishing him. Second Chronicles is the historic account of the calamity that came upon God's people when they disobeyed God and rejected His protection. And poor Isaiah was a great prophet, burdened by the intimate knowledge of how God's people would bring themselves to ruin, yet again. He foretold the future disobedience of God's people, and the subsequent devastations they would incur when they wandered far from God. But Isaiah also prophesied God would rescue His people.

All of these Scripture verses depict ruin. But the story doesn't end there. God followed all of the ruin with restoration, with rescue.

Addiction is hard to quantify. Where did it come from? Whose fault is it? Where does my choice end and my disease begin? Where does my disease end and my choice take over? God simply asks you to admit your complete defeat and enter into His rescue mission for you. God promised He would visit His humble people with healing and care. He keeps that promise every day.

Look over the words and phrases which stood out to you. Let the words be alive in your heart. What do you think Your Father God is saying to you? What is the Holy Spirit stirring in your heart?

Write your thoughts as a prayer:

Share with the group, if you want to.

<u>Step 1 Proclamation</u>
God rescues.

Step 2

I came to believe that a Power greater than myself could restore me to sanity.

Reality: Power
Principles: Belief, Hope

Nature is full of all kinds of powers that are greater than myself. Floods, earthquakes, and cyclones are all powers much greater than I. But those greater powers tend to destroy. They don't restore, and they certainly can't restore *me*. Impersonal forces that have no capacity to care, or to not care, about *me*.

There are other greater powers in the world that could, under the right circumstances, help restore a person to sanity. A loving family and a caring community may be able to help someone regain clear thinking and life-affirming choices. But for now, I'm beyond those options. Either addiction has robbed me of family and community, or addiction has caused me so much ruination that my family and community can't help me.

My troubles are big; I need a power much greater than I. Also, I need a greater power Who *wants* to help me.

I see that God has helped others. I think I am worse: maybe I've ruined my chances with God. But others assure me; He wants to help me and He can. So I'm coming to believe in God's power, I'm coming to believe He is able to help me. And I'm coming to believe in God's goodness. I'm beginning to believe what others are telling me about God; He will help me—if I seek Him.

We pray: Heavenly Father, Abba, Your Word is alive. Let Your Word be alive in me. Come Holy Spirit. In Jesus' name I pray. Amen.

Read the Scripture verses slowly:

Job 12:10   In his hand is the soul of every living thing, and the life breath of all mortal flesh.

What word or phrase stands out to me?

Isaiah 41:17-18   The afflicted and the needy seek water in vain, their tongues are parched with thirst. I, the LORD, will answer them; I, the God of Israel, will not forsake them.

What word or phrase stands out to me?

Isaiah 41:13   For I am the LORD, your God, who grasp your right hand; It is I who say to you, Do not fear, I will help you.

What word or phrase stands out to me?

Job 8:6   Should you be blameless and upright, surely
now he will rouse himself for you and restore
your rightful home.

What word or phrase stands out to me?

So much of Old Testament Scripture is about God restoring His people to wholeness and blessedness; it's about God promising restoration. It's about God keeping His promises. But why is there so much restoration in Scripture?

There are two reasons for this:

The first reason is about the people themselves. God's people rejected Him and strayed from Him so often, they seemed to be in constant need of help.

The second reason is about God. God *wants* to restore his people. He loves us even in our self-ruination. We are His beloved.

All through history, people have been surprised at how thoroughly they can ruin themselves, but God is never surprised. He always and forever knows just how far His people would stray, just how low His people would fall, just how broken His people would become. He always knows how much his people would resist His help. When God promises restoration, He knows what that means, He knows what it will take.

Look over the words and phrases which stood out to you. Let the words be alive in your heart. What do you think Your Father God is saying to you? What is the Holy Spirit stirring in your heart?

Write your thoughts as a prayer:

Share with the group, if you want to.

Step 2 Proclamation
God loves me.
He is powerful to help me.

Step 3

I made a decision to turn my will and my life over to the care of God as I understood Him.

Reality: Rescue, Now
Principle: Submission, Trust, Humility

If a parent is faithful, and steady, and caring, the child will trust she is safe. She will more readily seek her parent's advice. She will more readily obey her parent's word. If the parent is good, the child trusts that goodness.

I'm uncomfortable with that. I don't trust anyone well enough to turn myself over to their direction or care. My life has been hard. People have broken my trust. And sometimes it seemed that God didn't care about me either. So turning my will and life over to His care — that may be too much to ask.

But part of me thinks: I've already lost so much, I may not have much left to lose — why not try and see what happens? And, still, another part of me thinks: What if, *what if,* God really does know what's best for me? What if God really does want to make me well? *What if?*

Even though I feel scared, something in my heart makes me want to turn my will, my life, *my whole self,* over to God. People tell me that God can be trusted with my will and my life. People tell me the very fact that I'm here is proof. "There's no such thing as coincidence," they say. I'm not alive by some crazy accident. I'm here because God kept me here. I'm in recovery because God brought me to recovery. What I do with that is my choice, but that's what people are telling me: "God brought you here." Something in my heart is saying He *really will* care for me, He *really will* guide me. Is that 'Something' God Himself? If that 'something' is God Himself, any truthful understanding of Him must come from Him. He must show me who He is. He must show me how I ought to understand Him.

We pray: Heavenly Father, Abba, Your Word is alive. Let Your Word be alive in me. Come Holy Spirit. In Jesus' name I pray. Amen.

Read the Scripture verses slowly:

John 14:23 Jesus answered and said to him, "Whoever loves me will keep my word, and my Father will love him, and we will come to him and make our dwelling with him.

What word or phrase stands out to me?

Deuteronomy 5:13 Be careful, therefore, to do as the LORD, your God, has commanded you, not turning aside to the right or to the left, but following exactly the way that the LORD, your God, commanded you that you may live and prosper, and may have long life in the land which you are to possess.

What word or phrase stands out to me?

Psalm 23:1-2

The LORD is my shepherd; there is nothing I lack. In green pastures he makes me lie down; to still waters he leads me, he restores my soul. He guides me along right paths for the sake of his name.

What word or phrase stands out to me?

The Bible recounts many episodes of disobedience. From the very first time people sinned, they demonstrated a distrust of God's goodness and caring. Thought they knew better than God. People wanted to be their own gods and ignore the One True God. They were steeped in their own pride and defiance.

But other times in Scripture, people obeyed God. Sometimes they obeyed because they were afraid to bring upon themselves the same kinds of bad consequences as they had experienced previously. But other times, the people obeyed God because they remembered His goodness and they trusted His guidance.

I want to have the humility to obey God because I trust His goodness and guidance. That would be a new experience for me. God only wants me to start where I am right now. He wants me to trust that my past does not have to be my future. He wants me to trust Him here. Now.

Look over the words and phrases which stood out to you. Let the words be alive in your heart. What do you think Your Father God is saying to you? What is the Holy Spirit stirring in your heart?

Write your thoughts as a prayer:

Share with the group, if you want to.

<u>Step 3 Proclamation</u>
God loves me. He is worthy of my trust.

Step 4

I made a searching and fearless moral inventory of myself.

Reality: Sin
Principles: Honesty, Humility, Bravery

"I was wrong." Those words might be the hardest words for anyone to say. To admit to myself my own *wrong-doings* is painful. To know and admit my own *faults* is harrowing. It wounds my ego.

If I think about it, I can see that this is typical for human beings. I can see evidence all around me of problems caused by people refusing to see their own shortcomings and faults. So I'm tempted to just shrug my shoulders and say, "Well, everyone's like this. There's nothing to be done about it."

But there *is* something that can be done about it. I can begin to change that destructive habit in myself. I can begin to be honest about my weaknesses and faults. I can begin to be honest about my sins. But I can also begin to be honest about my strengths and talents.

What would it be like if I stopped hiding behind my ego and really started to look at myself? Would the truth really set me free? Would I discover in me some strengths and attributes that have been hidden? Would I uncover defects and faults that I can begin to work on?

We pray: Heavenly Father, Abba, Your Word is alive. Let Your Word be alive in me. Come Holy Spirit. In Jesus' name I pray. Amen.

Read the Scripture verses slowly:

Psalm 139:23-24   God, know my heart; try me, know my thoughts. See if there is a wicked path in me; lead me along an ancient path...

What word or phrase stands out to me?

Psalm 38:4-5   There is no wholesomeness in my flesh because of your anger; there is no health in my bones because of my sin. My iniquities overwhelm me, a burden too heavy for me.

What word or phrase stands out to me?

2 Corinthians 7:9-10   ...because you were saddened into repentance; for you were saddened in a godly way, so that you did not suffer loss in anything because of us. For godly sorrow produces a salutary repentance without regret, but worldly sorrow produces death.

What word or phrase stands out to me?

Psalm 139:14-15   You formed my inmost being; you knit me in my mother's womb. I praise you, because I am wonderfully made; wonderful are your works! My very self you know.

What word or phrase stands out to me?

The one hundred fifty Psalms of King David are wonderful prayers. Many of them were written as songs because King David was a musician. In the Psalms, we can find a prayer for every human emotion, for every human condition, for every human experience. There are Psalms asking God for protection against harm. In some, the psalmist wonders if God is near, or if He has abandoned them? Some Psalms are prayers repenting of sin. Some Psalms rejoice in God's presence and providence and rescue.

Sometimes I think my experiences are so unique – that I am alone in my struggles. In the Psalms I see something different. I see that for thousands of years, human beings have struggled with the same things I struggle with today. In the Psalms I see that God came to the help of his people; God comes to the help of His people today. In the Psalms I see that the human experiences, emotions, perceptions, and moods are always changing, but God's goodness and power never falters, it never changes. God is here. He knows me. I can be honest and humble and vulnerable with God.

Look over the words and phrases which stood out to you. Let the words be alive in your heart. What do you think Your Father God is saying to you? What is the Holy Spirit stirring in your heart?

Write your thoughts as a prayer:

Share with the group, if you want to.

<u>Step 4 Proclamation:</u>
God loves me. He knows me.
He helps me to love myself.

NOTES

Step 5

I admitted to God, to myself, and to another human being the exact nature of my wrongs.

Reality: Confession, Admission
Principles: Honesty, Bravery

Fourteen hundred years ago, Saint Augustine wrote, "The confession of evil works is the first beginning of good works."

Augustine was a sinner who created many years of wreckage. But he experienced a personal encounter with Jesus. Because of that encounter, he turned his life over to the care of God, and he eventually became a great saint. Augustine had to know from experience how hard confessing wrong-doings and defects is, because had so many bad actions and faults to confess.

Sometimes in our culture, people 'overshare.' TMI (Too Much Information) is like the common cold—it's easily contagious and everyone is susceptible. But the fifth step is not like that. The fifth step is honest and intentional. I'm beginning to want goodness in my life; I'm not hiding out any more, but I deserve to be careful with this step.

So I prayerfully ask God: Have You put the right person in my life to whom I can admit my faults and failures? Lord, will You put that person in my life? I humbly ask you to. God, when I am face to face with that person, will You help me to remember that I'm admitting my sins *first and foremost*, to You, who loves me? Will You let me experience the freedom and joy of no longer hiding from the entire human race? Will You give me the peace to be Your beloved and accepted?

Lord God, You love me just the way I am, and You love me *too much* to leave me just the way I am. The fifth step is real evidence of this truth.

We pray: Heavenly Father, Abba, Your Word is alive. Let Your Word be alive in me. Come Holy Spirit. In Jesus' name I pray. Amen.

Read the Scripture verses slowly:

Psalm 32:3-5

When I kept silent, my bones wasted away through my groaning all day long. For day and night your hand was heavy on me; my strength was sapped as in the heat of summer. Then I acknowledged my sin to you and did not cover up my iniquity. I said, "I will confess my transgressions to the Lord." And you forgave the guilt of my sin.

What word or phrase stands out to me?

1 John 1:9

If we acknowledge our sins, he is faithful and just and will forgive our sins and cleanse us from every wrongdoing.

What word or phrase stands out to me?

Matthew 3:6   ...and they (people in the crowd) were being baptized by him in the Jordan River as they acknowledged their sins

What word or phrase stands out to me?

James 5:16   Therefore, confess your sins to one another and pray for one another, that you may be healed. The fervent prayer of a righteous person is very powerful.

What word or phrase stands out to me?

When the Son of God, Jesus, came into the world in the flesh, He proclaimed that the time of preparation and waiting was over. God would, through Jesus, rescue the human race. Jesus is the Father's rescue mission, come in the flesh. This was astonishingly good news.

The New Testament Gospel recounts that *each person* who heard the Good News (the rescue mission of God) was called to do two things. They were called to repentance, that is, the humble confession of sin and turning away from sin. And they were called to believe in Jesus.

The apostle John wrote the Gospel of John, but he also wrote letters (epistles) to believers. In his writings, we see his intimate friendship with Jesus. John was transformed by the Person of Jesus Christ. John was a rescued man.

Sometimes you and I want to keep our friends for ourselves. This isn't so with John; he knew that Jesus commissioned him to invite you and me into deep, intimate friendship with Jesus, too. An intimate friend is someone who knows you deeply and who loves you faithfully. The fifth step is where an intimate friendship with Jesus begins. I tell Him what He already knows is true about me. I admit what's true and I enter an intimate friendship with Him.

Look over the words and phrases which stood out to you. Let the words be alive in your heart. What do you think Your Father God is saying to you? What is the Holy Spirit stirring in your heart?

Write your thoughts as a prayer:

Share with the group, if you want to.

<u>Step 5 Proclamation</u>
God loves me. He forgives me.

Step 6

**I was entirely ready to have God remove
all these defects of character.**

Reality: Burden
Principles: Acceptance, Hope

Chaos is easy to do and hard to live. Change is hard to do and easy to live.

Am I entirely ready to have God remove all the sinful ugliness from me? That sounds like I may be on the brink of a very profound change. Change can begin right here and now. But change will probably be a process that continues through my whole life.

But, I'm not just ready for *any* change. I'm not just interested in some kind of reinvention of myself. I want redemption. I want to change *in God*. The ancient Christian Church called this now-and-onward process of changing in God "metanoia."

Metanoia cannot happen unless I trust God. He calls me His beloved. Metanoia is impossible unless I welcome God's tender, powerful love for me. But. If I *really* believe I'm God's beloved child, if I *really* trust that He is awesomely good, every good thing is possible.

I look to the Cross. I see what God the Father gave to heal broken me. I see what He gave to rescue me. He gave His Son, Jesus. The Father gave His Son so that I would also be called His child—His healed and rescued child.

I will pray, "Lord, help me to trust you. Help me to look back through these Scriptures and see the Truth: Your whole heart is set upon rescuing Your people. Your whole heart is set upon rescuing me, right here, right now. Amen."

We pray: Heavenly Father, Abba, Your Word is alive. Let Your Word be alive in me. Come Holy Spirit. In Jesus' name I pray. Amen.

Read the Scripture verses slowly:

Matthew 4:17

From that time on, Jesus began to preach and say, "Repent, for the kingdom of heaven is at hand."

What word or phrase stands out to me?

Luke 5:31-32

Jesus said to them in reply, "Those who are healthy do not need a physician, but the sick do. I have not come to call the righteous to repentance but sinners.

What word or phrase stands out to me?

Acts 3:19

Repent, therefore, and be converted, that your sins may be wiped away...

What word or phrase stands out to me?

2 Corinthians 3: 18   And we all, with unveiled face, beholding the glory of the Lord, are being transformed into the same image from one degree of glory to another. For this comes from the Lord who is the Spirit.

What word or phrase stands out to me?

These New Testament Scripture passages continue with the theme of repentance—of turning away from sin toward God. In the passage from Corinthians, the theme of turning toward God intensifies—it becomes *transformation*.

Sometimes we misunderstand repentance in Scripture. Sometimes people think repentance is a way to make ourselves loveable to God, or we think repentance is a way to convince God to love us. But that's wrong thinking. I never have to try and convince God to love me. He already does, forever and unbreakably. *Nothing I can do will make God not love me!* Nothing I can do will make God take back His loving rescue. God will not change His mind about me. I am His beloved child.

Repentance is not to make God love me. Repentance is the way by which I begin to *receive* God's awesome love. It's a choice to return and receive. In repentance, I turn away from my sin, I turn my face to God. I say, "I'm sorry I turned away from You, Lord. I reach out my hands to receive You, and in Your goodness, You draw me close to Your heart. Transform me. Amen."

Look over the words and phrases which stood out to you. Let the words be alive in your heart. What do you think Your Father God is saying to you? What is the Holy Spirit stirring in your heart?

Write your thoughts as a prayer:

Share with the group, if you want to.

<u>Step 6 Proclamation</u>
God loves me. He is here with me in this moment.

Step 7

I humbly asked Him to remove my shortcomings.

Reality: Unburden, Release
Principles: Humility, Trust, Willingness

"That's just me." "That's just the way I am." I've said this about myself often, usually with a sense of defiance, sometimes with a sense of defeat. I flaunt my defects: my exasperation, my short-temperedness, rudeness, and gossip, and I offer no apology to anyone. Zero. If people don't like it, they can get lost. Or maybe I do the opposite. Maybe I decide that defects like my insecurities and clinginess are so repulsive, I don't blame anyone for running the other way. Either way, my defects have been almost immoveable forces. I hardly expect them to change.

But in Step 6 I became ready to have God remove all this. Even though I'm not sure I really expect Him to, in Step 7, I humbly ask Him.

Step 7 is where the next-level miracles start happening. I ask God to remove all my shortcomings; with my participation, He does. I tell Him impatience is a real problem for me; then, God removes insecurity over my finances. I ask God to remove my laziness as a parent; He gives me opportunities to practice motivation, and in the meantime, He begins removing my lust. I ask God to remove my resentments over my failed marriage; He does that, and He begins to remove my irresponsibility with money. I humbly ask God to remove my dishonesty at work, and all of a sudden, I no longer enjoy gossip.

I humbly ask God to remove my shortcomings and He does; in the order and to the degree that He deems best for me right now. I'm learning to trust that God wants to help me, and that He knows how best to help me. The more I live in Him, the more I want to live in Him. Metanoia continues. My relationship with the Lord deepens. Little by little, He makes me more and more like Jesus.

God loves me exactly the way I am. And He loves me too much to leave me exactly the way I am. Experiencing this truth is giving me joy.

We pray: Heavenly Father, Abba, Your Word is alive. Let Your Word be alive in me. Come Holy Spirit. In Jesus' name I pray. Amen.

Read the Scripture verses slowly:

Hebrews 4:16   So let us confidently approach the throne of grace to receive mercy and to find grace for timely help.

What word or phrase stands out to me?

Ephesians 2:4-5   But God, who is rich in mercy, because of the great love he had for us, even when we were dead in our transgressions, brought us to life with Christ (by grace you have been saved)...

What word or phrase stands out to me?

Titus 2:11-14   For the grace of God has appeared, saving all and training us to reject godless ways and worldly desires and to live temperately, justly, and devoutly in this age, as we await the blessed hope, the appearance of the glory of the great God and of our savior Jesus Christ, who gave himself for us to deliver us from all lawlessness and to cleanse for himself a people as his own, eager to do what is good.

What word or phrase stands out to me?

1 Corinthians 10:13   No trial has come to you but what is human. God is faithful and will not let you be tried beyond your strength; but with the trial he will also provide a way out, so that you may be able to bear it.

What word or phrase stands out to me?

Four hundred years before Augustine (mentioned in Step 4), there was Paul of Tarsus. Paul was a highly respected and committed scholar of the Law of Moses. He lived during the time of the early Christian community. Paul had not met Jesus before the Crucifixion, but in a very powerful and personal way, Paul did meet Jesus later.

At Pentecost, upon the unleashing of the Holy Spirit, the community of Christian believers grew. It kept growing. The Apostles went about preaching the Good News of Jesus. Paul vehemently opposed this movement. He persecuted Christian believers. Paul assisted at the murder of the first Christian martyr, Stephen (recounted in Acts of the Apostles chapter 7.) It's hard to imagine that a man who was an accomplice to murder became a disciple of the Lord. But he did. Paul encountered Jesus; he repented of his evil, and he became a committed follower of the Lord.

We should find real comfort and encouragement in this astonishing conversion.

Paul became a great disciple of Jesus. He spread the Gospel of Jesus to many people. Altogether, fourteen letters of the New Testament have been attributed to St Paul of Tarsus (or to his disciples). In these letters, Paul wrote to local churches or to individual disciples, encouraging them, correcting them, and inspiring them to follow Jesus more fully.

Paul never referred to the believers of Jesus as "Christians." Instead, he referred to them as "saints." Paul corrected saints!

We should find real comfort and encouragement in this! The saints whom Paul corrected weren't perfect, just as we aren't perfect. The saints were believers in Jesus who humbly received correction from Paul, because they knew the correction was really from God.

If you believe that Jesus is Lord, if you are turning from sin and toward God, and if you receive correction with humility, then you, too, are a saint.

How is it *even possible* that you went from being an active addict to being a saint?

You've been rescued. Jesus rescued you.

Jesus took your addiction; He took your sins; He took on the harm you've done and all the hurt you've ever experienced. He took it all *into* Himself and He took it all *to* the Cross. Everything that ruins you, everything that was killing you, He let it kill Him. Everything that drags you to the grave put Him in the grave.

And then He beat it. He trounced it. He took all that sin, all that harm, into the grave and *He left it there*. He rose, alive and victorious. He did that so you could be rescued. He did that so you could be healed. Jesus wants you to *receive* the victory that is His life. *That's* what grace is: God pouring His victorious life into you.

God's grace. You didn't earn it. Your only task is to *believe* in Him who gives it, to *turn* to Him who gives it, to *receive* what He gives you, to always *ask* Him for more, and to *live* in His victorious life.

Look over the words and phrases which stood out to you. Let the words be alive in your heart. What do you think Your Father God is saying to you? What is the Holy Spirit stirring in your heart?

Write your thoughts as a prayer:

Share with the group, if you want to.

<u>Step 7 Proclamation</u>
God loves me. Only He can transform me and heal me.

NOTES

Step 8

I made a list of all persons I had harmed and became willing to make amends to them all.

Reality: Harm
Principles: Discipline, Humility, Accountability

So far, this process has been hard. But I've been surrounded by people who want me to succeed. Some of my supporters have never experienced or suffered from my addiction. Some people whom I have harmed *still* wish me well. I see their support as an unearned gift. Then, there are some people who have bitter feelings against me. Some of them are really justified.

My Heavenly Father is doing something miraculous in me. He is rescuing me from my addiction; He rescued me from sin; and He's even rescuing me from my worst inclinations and defects. He loves me. I am seen, known, and loved by God.

It's only because I'm loved that I can make this list of all people I have harmed. I know God is helping me. I trust He'll keep helping me. He's with me in this moment. I remember that each of the persons I have harmed, Jesus died in their place, too. Jesus took all their harm and hurt onto the cross, too.

People have been harmed by my actions, my selfishness, my cruelty, my addiction. I can't do much to make it right, but Jesus can. In my heart, I feel Jesus is saying, "I *died* for these people. Can you *live*, at least through this step, for these people?"

I am loved by God. He wants to do a new mighty work: He wants to love me through this difficult step.

We pray: Heavenly Father, Abba, Your Word is alive. Let Your Word be alive in me. Come Holy Spirit. In Jesus' name I pray. Amen.

Read the Scripture verses slowly:

Psalm 133:1-3   How good and how pleasant it is, when brothers dwell together as one!

What word or phrase stands out to me?

John 13:34-35   I give you a new commandment: love one another. As I have loved you, so you also should love one another. This is how all will know that you are my disciples, if you have love for one another.

What word or phrase stands out to me?

Matthew 5:22   But I say to you, whoever is angry with his brother will be liable to judgment...

What word or phrase stands out to me?

Matthew 5:9   Blessed are the peacemakers, for they shall be called sons of God.

What word or phrase stands out to me?

Matthew 5:44   But I say to you, love your enemies, and pray for those who persecute you...

What word or phrase stands out to me?

Three of the Gospels are very similar. These three, Matthew, Mark and Luke, are called the synoptic Gospels. That means that they are from the same (syn) point of view (optic). They tell the story of Jesus' ministry—His three years of teaching, miracles and preaching, followed by His death and resurrection. (John tells the story from a different perspective: he tells much more of the spiritual realities hidden inside the events.) The Gospel of Matthew was probably the first Gospel written (as early as 40 AD and as late as 80 AD.) Matthew wrote in Greek for a Christian and Jewish audience. His Gospel is filled with references to customs that would have been very familiar to Jewish people. Matthew's Gospel includes seven narrative sections, wherein Matthew recounts Jesus' works, and five lengthy discourse sections, in which Jesus reveals that the Kingdom of God is at hand, and in which He teaches the people how to live.

In the early Church, the Gospel of Matthew was used more than the others for instructing Christians. We can see in the Scriptures for Step 8, especially in the quotes from the Gospel of Matthew, Jesus taught His disciples to be peaceful among others, to make amends, and to seek unity whenever possible.

Look over the words and phrases which stood out to you. Let the words be alive in your heart. What do you think Your Father God is saying to you? What is the Holy Spirit stirring in your heart?

Write your thoughts as a prayer:

Share with the group, if you want to.

<u>Step 8 Proclamation</u>
God loves me.
He is the God of peace.

Step 9

I made direct amends to such people wherever possible, except when to do so would injure them or others.

Reality: Repair
Principles: Honesty, Bravery, Peacefulness

This process of making amends is proposed in two distinct steps. I'm grateful for that. I need time to work through this all. I need support. I need time to pray. I need the living Word of God, the God who loves me and speaks to me. I need all His help and grace to be able to do what I'm about to do.

Jesus said we're supposed to forgive people "seven times seventy times" if they express sorrow for their wrongs. That number isn't meant to be specific; it actually means an unspecified, unending amount of times. I don't think I want anyone to forgive me an unending amount of times, I just want them to forgive me *this one time*-this one time I approach them and say "I am truly sorry for harming you. God is really helping me to change. Please forgive me." I hope people will understand.

The people who support me have warned me not to argue with anyone when working this step. I can be at peace. I can say my piece and go away. Even though God has instructed us *all* in forgiveness, I realize the people I have harmed owe me nothing. Their responses ultimately belong to them and to God.

This work God is doing in me — His rescue — is between God and me. No matter what happens, I can go away from making amends knowing God loves me *and* He loves the person to whom I offer amends.

If I'm worried my amends would harm the person or others involved, I pray for God's guidance. God may direct me to talk it over with someone I trust and who supports me. I'm grateful to know where to turn when I'm unsure how to proceed.

God has rescued each of us — the person I owe amends, and me. *Lord, send me your grace. Send your grace to the person I approach today. Let me not forget Who you are. Let me not forget who I am to You. In Jesus' name. Amen.*

We pray: Heavenly Father, Abba, Your Word is alive. Let Your Word be alive in me. Come Holy Spirit. In Jesus' name I pray. Amen.

Read the Scripture verses slowly:

Matthew 5: 23-24   Therefore, if you bring your gift to the altar, and there recall that your rother has anything against you, leave your gift there at the altar, go first and be reconciled with your brother, and then come and offer your gift.

What word or phrase stands out to me?

Romans 12:18-19, 21   If possible, on your part, live at peace with all. Do not be conquered by evil but conquer evil with good.

What word or phrase stands out to me?

Ephesians 4:31-32   All bitterness, fury, anger, shouting, and reviling must be removed from you, along with all malice. [And] be kind to one another, compassionate, forgiving one another as God has forgiven you in Christ.

What word or phrase stands out to me?

Hebrews 12:14   Strive for peace with everyone, and for that holiness without which no one will see the Lord.

What word or phrase stands out to me?

Every word of the New Testament is a word of instruction to me. Paul wrote the letter to the Romans in the winter of A.D. 58. He probably wrote to the people of Ephesus in about A.D. 62 from a Roman prison cell. The letter to Hebrews was probably written by someone in Paul's inner circle, but it accurately reflects Paul's teaching and guidance. It was written to correct Roman Christians who were considering abandoning their belief in Jesus and going back to their old ways of life. I read these instructions and I'm certain I need every word of it.

I'm certain that God, Who loves me and Who is rescuing me *for* Himself, is in every word speaking to me. Every word is alive.

God is so generous. He has given me a circle of people who care about my progress. Not all of them are in recovery. God has given me a circle of people who proclaim His Holy word to me, a circle of people who remind me I am loved. Here's the most astonishing thing: I'm beginning to share the Good News back to them, too. I'm beginning to encourage, remind, and lift up others. I never thought I would be useful to another person. God's grace is making me useful to others.

Now I'm going to take some quiet time to remember all that God has done for me so far. My heart is beginning to be filled with peace, joy, and gratitude. I say to the Father, "Please send your Holy Spirit. Come Holy Spirit. In Jesus' name I ask. Amen." This is what freedom feels like. God has rescued me *for* freedom; He has rescued me for the freedom of His love.

Look over the words and phrases which stood out to you. Let the words be alive in your heart. What do you think Your Father God is saying to you? What is the Holy Spirit stirring in your heart?

Write your thoughts as a prayer:

Share with the group, if you want to.

<u>Step 9 Proclamation</u>
God loves me.
He restores me.

Step 10

I continued to take personal inventory and when I was wrong promptly admitted it.

Reality: Growth
Principles: Acceptance, Honesty

Another day has gone by that I have not hidden from anybody. I am free. I am free to ask my Heavenly Father to pour out His Holy Spirit on me. I am free to ask this in Jesus' Holy Name. I am free to receive everything He wants to give me. He always wants to give me more of Himself.

I'm beginning to understand humility. Humility is honesty about my own *utter need for God,* and it is *trust in His power.* It is God's desire to help me. I need God in everything. God wants to help me in everything. I ask and I receive and I thank him. That is humility.

I want to always trust my Heavenly Father. I want to always be close to Jesus, to talk to Him, to listen as He speaks in my heart. I want to always be wide open and receptive to the Holy Spirit. The only way I can do this is to continue, with God's help, to check myself. Are my motives pure? Am I humble, or is pride creeping in? I look back to Steps 6 and 7 and I ask God to show me where and which of my defects are evident. Where do I still need to change?

This time it's not as hard because here, in Step 10, I trust God. I thank Him. I want more and more to do His will. I want more and more to receive His grace, which is His victorious life in me. I never expected this. God is giving me so much more than I ever imagined.

We pray: Heavenly Father, Abba, Your Word is alive. Let Your Word be alive in me. Come Holy Spirit. In Jesus' name I pray. Amen.

Read the Scripture verses slowly:

Psalm 51:12   A clean heart create for me, God; renew within me a steadfast spirit.

What word or phrase stands out to me?

John 15:4   Remain in me, as I remain in you. Just as a branch cannot bear fruit on its own unless it remains on the vine, so neither can you unless you remain in me.

What word or phrase stands out to me?

1 Kings 2:3   Keep the mandate of the LORD, your God, walking in his ways and keeping his statutes, commands, ordinances, and decrees as they are written in the Law of Moses, that you may succeed in whatever you do, and wherever you turn...

What word or phrase stands out to me?

Hebrews 13: 9   Do not be carried away by all kinds of strange teaching. It is good to have our hearts strengthened by grace...

What word or phrase stands out to me?

All through history and recounted in Scripture, human persons have brought themselves to ruin. And through it all, God has been breaking into history to rescue human persons from their ruin.

Some people have allowed God to rescue them. Some have lived in obedience to God and in gratitude for His rescue. I am becoming that someone. I want to remain that someone! My 12 Step recovery program reminds me to live "one day at a time." Scripture reminds me that God is in every moment of every day so I don't have to worry. I don't have to dwell on my past; God has already rescued me from that. I don't have to be anxious about my future; God my Father will meet me there when I get there. Right now, I'm here and He is here with me. Now.

I can look with courage and honesty at *me*, right now. God will help me. God is helping me.

Look over the words and phrases which stood out to you. Let the words be alive in your heart. What do you think Your Father God is saying to you? What is the Holy Spirit stirring in your heart?

Write your thoughts as a prayer:

Share with the group, if you want to.

<u>Step 10 Proclamation</u>
God loves me.
He grows me.

Step 11

I sought through prayer and meditation to improve my conscious contact with God as I understood Him, praying only for knowledge of His will for me and the power to carry that out.

Reality: Prayer
Principles: Commitment, Discipline, Humility

A good conversation requires honest talking and earnest listening. Prayer can be the best kind of conversation. I start my day by thanking my Father for calling me to prayer. If I'm praying, it's because I'm responding to my Farther calling me. Prayer is always God's idea first. He says, "Come, My beloved child, come talk with Me." It's always His idea. So He calls me to prayer and I offer my day to God to do with me whatever He wants, to show me whatever work He wants me to do, to bring His love wherever I go. I tell my Heavenly Father that I am ready for Him to change me in whatever way He knows is best at this moment. I ask, and I trust that He will give me everything I need to do His will and His work.

Many times, God is calling me to be generous and encouraging to my support community. But if I'm paying attention, He is also calling me to bring His love to everyone I meet: the grocery store cashier, the waiter who's pouring my coffee, the teens playing basketball outside in the street, the table server at the soup kitchen. All of these people are God's beloved—whether they know it or not. He wants me to view each of them in His truth. He wants *me* to be *evidence* of His love. Throughout the day I say to Him, "Remind me, Lord. Remind me. Come Holy Spirit. In Jesus' Holy Name I pray. Amen."

At the end of the day I return to Him, with committed time set aside, to talk and listen. I listen to the words He puts in my heart. I listen to the Word He tells me in Scripture. I listen to His Word. I let His Word change me; I let it transform me. The Father has so much work to do in me and with me. Still, I feel Him transforming me little by little to be more like His Son, Jesus. I'm beginning to understand the true meaning of the word *awesome*. That's Who God is—awesome. I'm beginning to understand the true meaning of the word *hope*. That's what I have in my heart.

We pray: Heavenly Father, Abba, Your Word is alive. Let Your Word be alive in me. Come Holy Spirit. In Jesus' name I pray. Amen.

Read the Scripture verses slowly:

1 Thessalonians 5:17 Pray without ceasing...

What word or phrase stands out to me?

1 John 5:14 And we have this confidence in him, that if we ask anything according to his will, he hears us.

What word or phrase stands out to me?

1 Chronicles 16:11-12 Rely on the mighty LORD; constantly seek his face. Recall the wondrous deeds he has done, his signs, and his words of judgment...

What word or phrase stands out to me?

Ephesians 6:18 With all prayer and supplication, pray at every opportunity in the Spirit. To that end, be watchful with all perseverance and supplication for all the holy ones.

What word or phrase stands out to me?

Matthew 26:41   Watch and pray that you may not undergo the test.

What word or phrase stands out to me?

2 Corinthians 12:9-10   My grace is sufficient for you, for power is made perfect in weakness. I will rather boast most gladly of my weaknesses, in order that the power of Christ may dwell with me.

What word or phrase stands out to me?

Psalm 71:14-15   I will always hope in you and add to all your praise. My mouth shall proclaim your just deeds, day after day your acts of deliverance...

What word or phrase stands out to me?

How is it possible that the God of the universe wants to hear what I have to say? All of Scripture is proof that God is interested in me. God is a community of Persons—Father, Son and Spirit. He needs nothing, and He is never lonely—and yet, He is interested in the words, the heart, thoughts, ideas, desires, and praise of human persons!

Like a generous and patient father sits by his child's bedside and listens to the child recount her day, so God is with our prayers—yours and mine. We cannot tell Him anything He doesn't already know. We cannot ask Him for anything that He hasn't already foreseen. But He wants to hear us speak. He delights in our conversation.

Throughout Scripture we can see five basic types of prayer. We can remember these types of prayer by the acronym ACTS.

A is for Adoration. We tell God what is true about Him; He is good. He is beautiful. He is powerful. He is generous. We bring Him our heart, day, life, our *everything*; we offer ourselves to God as an act of adoration; we offer ourselves as an act of worship.

C is for Contrition and Communion: Contrition: We confess our sins. We ask His forgiveness. We make a firm commitment to amend, to re-orient our thoughts, words and deeds toward His love. In **Communion**, we ask God to continue to make us one with Him through His Son Jesus. We say, "Come Holy Spirit. Make me one with the Father and Son and with You. Amen." Sometimes in Communion, we may not even say anything. We may just sit with God, in His embrace.

T is for Thanksgiving. We are loved by God. He has rescued us. Throughout the day He has shown His presence. He has given us grace. He has helped us in tough situations. He calls us His own children. Mindful of this, we can't *stop* thanking Him.

S is for Supplication. That's an old-fashioned word for "Please." We bring our needs to God. Mostly we need the grace to know and do His will. We ask God to help other people. We name them. We tell God our concerns. If we start to feel anxious or resentful about someone for whom we're praying, we ask God, "Please help me to pray with a pure and peaceful heart."

Look over the words and phrases which stood out to you. Let the words be alive in your heart. What do you think Your Father God is saying to you? What is the Holy Spirit stirring in your heart?

Write your thoughts as a prayer:

Share with the group, if you want to.

<u>Step 11 Proclamation</u>
God loves me. He delights in my conversation with Him.
He guides me.

NOTES

Step 12

Having had a spiritual awakening as the result of these Steps, I tried to carry this message to addicts and to practice these principles in all my affairs.

Reality: Transformation
Principles: Service, Gratitude, Generosity

I had no idea that a "spiritual awakening" would mean I've entered into a relationship of love with God, my Creator and Father. I didn't know that a "spiritual awakening" would mean that I'd come to understand I've been rescued by the obedient sacrifice of Jesus, God the Son. I was completely unaware that "spiritual awakening" means I would be graced by God and filled with the Holy Spirit. How could I know that I'd *want* ever more of Him, that I'd *receive* ever more of Him? But that's what has happened. That's what God has done for me and in me.

How can I *not* share this news with others?

I've heard it said that evangelization is "one beggar telling another where to find bread." I've been rescued. I have found bread. And the Bread of Life, God Himself, has found me.

I will respect other people's boundaries. I will respect their decision to hear the Good News or to ignore it. I will practice humility, prudence, and integrity, making certain that my actions and demeanor reflect the Gospel I proclaim. But I will also embrace the astonishing and eternal Truth that we have been rescued by God. I will tell the truth.

We pray: Heavenly Father, Abba, Your Word is alive. Let Your Word be alive in me. Come Holy Spirit. In Jesus' name I pray. Amen.

Read the Scripture verses slowly:

Romans 8:14-15   For those who are led by the Spirit of God are children of God. For you did not receive a spirit of slavery to fall back into fear, but you received a spirit of adoption, through which we cry, "Abba, Father!

What word or phrase stands out to me?

Matthew 4:18   (Jesus) said to them, "Come after me, and I will make you fishers of men."

What word or phrase stands out to me?

Luke 19:40   (Jesus) said in reply, "I tell you, if they keep silent, the stones will cry out!"

What word or phrase stands out to me?

1 Corinthians 15:58   Therefore, my beloved brothers, be firm, steadfast, always fully devoted to the work of the Lord, knowing that in the Lord your labor is not in vain.

What word or phrase stands out to me?

Galatians 6:9   Let us not grow tired of doing good, for in due time we shall reap our harvest, if we do not give up... Be greatly encouraged.

What word or phrase stands out to me?

Hebrews 6:18-19   We have this hope as an anchor for the soul, firm and secure.

What word or phrase stands out to me?

Hebrews 13:3   Be mindful of prisoners as if sharing their imprisonment, and of the ill-treated as of yourselves, for you also are in the body.

What word or phrase stands out to me?

All through history God has been rescuing His people. All through history, God has been instructing His people to *remember* and to *proclaim*. Remember what God has done. Remember His mighty works. Remember His tender love. Remember His promises kept. Proclaim! Proclaim what God has done. Proclaim His mighty works. Proclaim His tender love. Proclaim His promises kept.

All throughout history, all throughout Scripture, God has rescued His people. I have been rescued by God. I will remember it with my every thought. I will live it with my every choice. I will proclaim it with my every word.

Look over the words and phrases which stood out to you. Let the words be alive in your heart. What do you think Your Father God is saying to you? What is the Holy Spirit stirring in your heart?

Write your thoughts as a prayer:

Share with the group, if you want to.

<u>Step 12 Proclamation</u>
God loves me. I love Him. I live in His love. I live in His truth.

Epilogue:

Then your light shall break forth like the dawn,
and your wound shall quickly be healed;

Your vindication shall go before you,

and the glory of the LORD shall be your rear guard.

Then you shall call, and the LORD will answer,
you shall cry for help, and he will say: "Here I am!"

If you remove the yoke from among you,

the accusing finger, and malicious speech;

If you lavish your food on the hungry
and satisfy the afflicted;

Then your light shall rise in the darkness,

and your gloom shall become like midday;

Then the LORD will guide you always
and satisfy your thirst in parched places,
will give strength to your bones

And you shall be like a watered garden,

like a flowing spring whose waters never fail.

Your people shall rebuild the ancient ruins;

the foundations from ages past you shall raise up;

"Repairer of the breach," they shall call you,

"Restorer of ruined dwellings."

Isaiah 38:8-12

May God be praised. Today, just for today, I ask God to give me the grace I need to seek Him, to entreat Him, to praise Him and to follow Him.

Today, just for today, I will live as the Person God made me to be. I am His.

I am rescued.

Amen.

APPENDIX

About our meetings:

Our meetings are not intended to be a 12 Step recovery how-to or to replace conventional 12 Step recovery meetings.

It isn't necessary that participants call themselves Christian.

Participants of all 12 Step recovery fellowships are welcome. People will come from different recovery groups and with different understandings of the Steps. People will embrace different definitions of what qualifies as "abstinent from addiction." At our meetings, we do not argue about any of these things. Instead, we receive others' perspective with a spirit of acceptance.

We confine our sharing to "I" statements and "God" statements. Crosstalk is reserved for the single purpose of identifying with another person's experience. Each of us shares our personal experiences, strength and hope. We believe others will learn more from this than from corrections or arguments.

We come together with different levels of familiarity and knowledge of the Bible. At our meetings, we don't teach Scripture, and we don't Bible surf. We confine our attention *only* to those Scriptures proposed in the chapter we're working. We do not argue about differences of interpretations. Of course, there are truer and less true understandings of God as he is revealed in Scripture, but our intention is to *enter into* the Living Word of God and to let His Word bring each of us into an ever-deepening encounter with Jesus Christ, God the Son.

Unlike typical 12 Step groups, "Rescue" groups don't count abstinence time. Our measure is whether we are working the Steps *today,* and whether we are meeting God in His Living word and in prayer *today.*

Finally, a word about sponsorship:

Typically, 12 Step recovery success relies heavily on the sponsor-sponsee relationship. *The Rescue: A 12 Step Bible Study*, is structured differently because most of us are not Bible scholars, priests, ordained ministers, or qualified spiritual directors. Even if members are, they do not function as that within the group. Therefore, we do not sponsor each other on the Rescue journey. Instead, we accompany each other; we pray together; we share our experiences of God rescuing us. We encourage people who want a formal guide through Scripture to seek out a validly qualified individual.

CPSIA information can be obtained
at www.ICGtesting.com
Printed in the USA
BVHW030955180819
556146BV00002B/184/P

9 781387 9291